A STRONG GIRLS' GUIDE TO BEING

TO EMMA AND GRACE, MY TWO STRONG GIRLS.

STERLING CHILDREN'S BOOKS
New York

An Imprint of Sterling Publishing Co., Inc.
1166 Avenue of the Americas
New York, NY 10036

Disclaimer: The author is not engaged in rendering professional advice or services to the individual reader. This book is not intended to be a substitute for the medical advice of a licensed physician. The reader should consult with their doctor in any matters relating to his/her health. The author shall not be liable or responsible for any loss or damages allegedly arising from any information or suggestion in this book.

ISBN 978-1-4549-3282-6

Distributed in Canada by Sterling Publishing Co., Inc.
c/o Canadian Manda Group, 664 Annette Street
Toronto, Ontario M6S 2C8, Canada
Distributed in the United Kingdom by GMC Distribution Services
Castle Place, 166 High Street, Lewes, East Sussex BN7 1XU, England
Distributed in Australia by NewSouth Books
University of New South Wales, Sydney, NSW 2052, Australia

For information about custom editions, special sales, and premium and corporate purchases, please contact Sterling Special Sales at 800-805-5489 or specialsales@sterlingpublishing.com.

Manufactured in China

Lot #:
2 4 6 8 10 9 7 5 3 1
06/19

sterlingpublishing.com

Cover design by Heather Kelly
Interior design by Julie Robine

PHOTO CREDITS
Getty Images: KaterinaKr: 54–55; slip lee: 83

A STRONG GIRLS' GUIDE TO BEING

EXERCISES AND INSPIRATION FOR BECOMING
A BRAVER, KINDER, HEALTHIER YOU

LANI SILVERSIDES
ILLUSTRATED BY REBECCA PRINN

STERLING CHILDREN'S BOOKS
New York

TABLE OF CONTENTS

"Don't ever underestimate the importance you can have, because history has shown us that courage can be contagious and hope can take on a life of its own."

MICHELLE OBAMA

INTRODUCTION

· ·

To the strong girls of the world . . .

   Yes, that's you! With the challenges of school, friends, family, and life in general—it can sometimes be easy to forget that you're worthy, beautiful, and capable of anything you set your mind to. Treat this guide as a journal about personal growth. In these pages, we'll practice positivity, mindfulness, compassion, and more. And at the end of the day, remember—practice does not make perfect. Practice makes progress. It's progress toward being the best, happiest, and strongest version of you.

   You are unstoppable. You've got this!

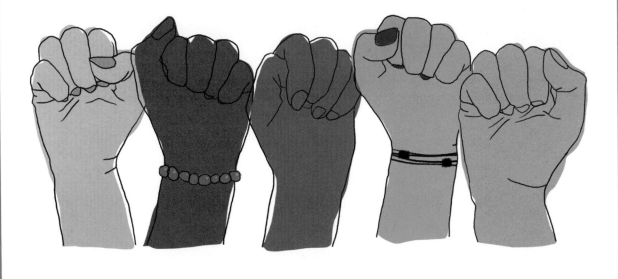

CHAPTER 1

I CAN BE Positive

"If you don't like something, change it.
If you can't change it, change your attitude."
MAYA ANGELOU

Positive emotions are like magnets for positive results. We have to work on developing positive emotions because our brains are actually wired with a bias towards negativity (yuck). When dealing with negative emotions, like fear or stress, our brain has been programmed to shut off all other things so that we can't even think about anything else. Not only does this make us unproductive, it can really put a damper on our mood and make us feel bad about ourselves.

That's why we need positivity! Positivity is like a reset button that puts the brakes on negativity. Positive emotions, such as joy, awe, and savoring small moments help you see new possibilities, which, in turn, give you the ability to build new skills such as recovering from setbacks, connecting with others, and boosting your self-confidence. Positivity can also improve your physical health and help you sleep better! The activities in this chapter will help you develop a more positive attitude and an outlook that brings joy to your daily life.

"It is what it is. But it will be what you make it."
PAT SUMMITT

Totally AWE-SOME

"Those who dwell among the beauties and mysteries
of the earth are never alone or weary of life."
RACHEL CARSON

Have you ever experienced something that made you pause or took your breath away? Maybe it was seeing your favorite musician live for the first time, or looking down from the top of the Empire State Building. Whatever it was, the word for this feeling is awe, as in when something is awesome, or when you are totally awestruck. This feeling is powerful. It can alter the way you process information, the way you think about what's going on around you, and even the way you see the world. It's been proven that noticing and understanding your own awe experiences can lead to better health and well-being. This is because knowing that the world is so huge and great can actually help you cope with difficult situations.

Awe can be found in the most ordinary of places. You can experience it by spending time outside in nature, volunteering in your community, listening to music, or just by breathing intentionally (more on breathing later).

· ·

When have you felt in awe of your surroundings? Describe one of these instances in the space below. Examples might include looking at the ocean or a mountain, or being on an airplane high above the ground.

_____

_____

_____

When have you felt part of something bigger than yourself? Describe one of these instances in the space below. Examples might include being at a sporting event or concert, or looking up at a clear sky full of stars.

_____

_____

_____

SMALL JOYS EQUALS BIG HAPPINESS

While awe can take the form of skydiving or a vacation to the Grand Canyon, it can also take more ordinary, smaller forms. In fact, it's better to try and notice the small moments in your day-to-day life that make you feel happy. The more time you take to notice these little details, the more your brain will start to pick up on these little gems all over the place, all the time.

Here are some small joys that people encounter daily. Circle the things you most identify as being awesome.

♡ Popping bubble wrap.

♡ Warm cookies right out of the oven.

♡ High-fiving babies.

♡ Wrapping up in a blanket on a cold day.

♡ Campfires.

♡ Jumping into a pool on a hot day.

♡ Falling asleep in the car and waking up when you get there.

♡ Peeling an orange in one go.

♡ Licking the cookie batter off the mixer.

♡ The first scoop out of a gallon of ice cream.

♡ Free samples of food in the grocery store.

♡ Air conditioning on a hot day.

♡ Finding money in the couch cushions or in a pocket.

♡ A baby's laugh.

♡ Getting that stubborn piece of popcorn out of your teeth.

♡ Spontaneous dance parties.

♡ Sneezing multiple times in a row.

♡ The moment before you go down on a roller coaster.

♡ Walking onto fresh snow.

♡ Sliding on your shoes without having to re-tie them.

♡ Snow days.

Now it's your turn! Make your own original list of the small but awesome occurrences in your daily life. Try to add at least one new item to the list each week.

MY ONGOING LIST OF *Awesome* & *Awe-inspiring* STUFF

_____

_____

_____

_____

_____

_____

_____

_____

_____

_____

SAVORING *Goodness*

The words savor or savoring are often used to talk about food, as in, "savoring a sweet dessert." But you can savor things other than food, too. Savoring just means noticing and appreciating the good in your life.

You can practice savoring a moment or a certain feeling by taking the time to notice what's happening around you. In order to truly savor something, you have to give it your full attention.

· ·

What are things you notice in nature that attract your attention? Waves crashing? Rainbows? Autumn leaves changing colors? Jot them down in the space below.

_____

_____

What are some smells, sounds, and physical sensations that stick out to you? Is it a clean shower after playing at the beach? How about the smell of your favorite meal being cooked? Jot them down in the space below.

_____

_____

You can savor memories, too! Think back to a happier time or moment. What made these things so special? Write about it in the space below.

_____

_____

_____

You can also savor the future. What are some things you have planned for the future that you are looking forward to? Jot them down in the space below.

_____

_____

_____

Last of all, you can savor the flaws and mishaps. Can you recall some times when things weren't perfect? What did you learn from these experiences? Write about it in the space below.

_____

_____

_____

Humor

Humor is another way we can bring more positive emotions into our life. Humor can even help us cope with the difficulties that we each face. Being humorous can mean making others laugh, telling or listening to jokes, or dancing in a silly way by yourself or in front of other people. Having a sense of humor can also mean finding the upside to our own mistakes so that we can move on and do better next time.

Who is someone that you consider humorous? This can be a comedian, an actor, or just someone you know who is hilarious. Describe what makes this person humorous in the space below.

_____

_____

_____

What are some things that make you laugh? Jot them down in the space below. Examples might include a comedic television show, a face your dog makes, or an inside joke between you and your friends.

_____

_____

_____

What are three things ways in which YOU are humorous? Do you crack jokes? Sing in a funny voice? Jot your funny moments down in the space below.

_____

_____

_____

In the space below, write about a time when something didn't go as planned, or when you made a mistake. Can you find humor in the situation?

_____

_____

_____

NEGATIVE FEELINGS NEED *Love*, TOO

Having a positive attitude doesn't always mean you will have positive emotions. Your attitude helps you understand your emotions in a healthy way, but that doesn't mean that you will always feel happy—and that's okay! Your negative feelings are a part of who you are, and there is nothing wrong with being angry, sad, worried, or even disappointed. The important thing is to recognize these feelings and be able to talk about them. When you're in touch with your negative feelings, you're more likely to accept them and be able to make a plan to turn your attention on what makes you feel better.

The first step to moving on from a negative feeling is to name it. Fill in the blanks below, matching the emotions with specific experiences that you've had.

I feel sad when _____

_____

I feel angry when _____

_____

I feel disappointed when _____

_____

I feel frustrated when _____

_____

I feel scared when _____

_____

I feel rotten when _____

_____

I feel annoyed when _____

_____

I feel confused when _____

_____

I feel jealous when _____

_____

I feel hopeless when _____

_____

Everyone deals with feelings differently. How do you manage your feelings? Fill in the blanks with actions or activities that help offset unpleasant emotions. These might include taking a deep breath, exercising, doing something creative, or telling someone you trust about how you feel.

· ·

When I feel upset, it helps if I _____

_____

_____

When I feel lonely, it helps if I _____

_____

_____

When I feel anxious, it helps if I _____

_____

_____

When I feel mad, it helps if I _____

_____

_____

When I feel frightened, it helps if I _____

_____

_____

When I feel irritated, it helps if I _____

_____

_____

When I feel hurt, it helps if I _____

_____

_____

When I feel uncomfortable, it helps if I _____

_____

_____

When I feel embarrassed, it helps if I _____

_____

_____

When I feel overwhelmed, it helps if I _____

_____

_____

CHAPTER 2

I CAN

Be Grateful

Gratitude is a feeling of being thankful and appreciative. You can do both, feel and show gratitude. When someone else shows us gratitude, such as thanking us for a gift or telling us how much they enjoy spending time together, it makes us feel all warm and fuzzy inside—but did you know that being grateful towards others, or just having an attitude of gratitude in general, also comes with tons of benefits? Feeling and expressing gratitude can:

- Increase happiness
- Put us in a better mood
- Build a stronger immune system (the system that protects us from getting sick!)
- Improve sleep
- Increase energy
- Help us be more empathetic, generous, and compassionate
- Lead to more optimism
- Help build strong relationships
- Allow for us to be more forgiving of ourselves and others
- Help us feel more positive emotions

Expressing gratitude is a powerful thing! Think of it as a renewable source of positivity and happiness. The following activities can help bring your attention to all the good in your life.

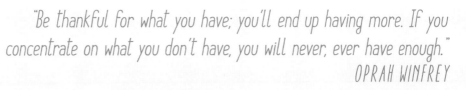

"Be thankful for what you have; you'll end up having more. If you concentrate on what you don't have, you will never, ever have enough."
OPRAH WINFREY

Gratitude Prompts

There are many things you can be grateful for. Write down some of your own by filling in the following blanks.

••

I'm grateful for_____ (family member),
because _____ .

I'm grateful for_____ (teacher),
because _____ .

I'm grateful for_____ (friend),
because _____ .

I'm grateful for_____ (something in nature),
because _____ .

Gratitude Lists

When we don't take the time to be grateful, we forget that our lives are made up of tiny joys and wonders. That's where lists come in handy!

- I'm grateful for these people in my life:_____
  _____
  _____

- I'm grateful for these activities:
  _____
  _____

- I'm grateful for these books:
  _____
  _____

- I'm grateful for these movies:
  _____
  _____

- I'm grateful for these foods:
  _____
  _____

- I'm grateful for these songs:
  _____
  _____
  _____

- I'm grateful for these weather conditions: _____
  _____
  _____

- I'm grateful for these moments in history: _____
  _____
  _____

- I'm grateful for these skills I have: _____
  _____
  _____

- I'm grateful for these places:
  _____
  _____

See? When you really put your mind to it, there's so much to appreciate!

THREE *Good* THINGS

Each night, write down three good things that happened during your day. This practice can help you feel grateful for all the little things in your life. Try it for the next few weeks here:

Wednesday ··········
1. _____
2. _____
3. _____

Sunday ················
1. _____
2. _____
3. _____

Thursday ···············
1. _____
2. _____
3. _____

Monday ···············
1. _____
2. _____
3. _____

Friday ················
1. _____
2. _____
3. _____

Tuesday ···············
1. _____
2. _____
3. _____

Saturday ···············
1. _____
2. _____
3. _____

Sunday ·················

1. _____

2. _____

3. _____

Thursday ···············

1. _____

2. _____

3. _____

Monday ·················

1. _____

2. _____

3. _____

Friday ···················

1. _____

2. _____

3. _____

Tuesday ················

1. _____

2. _____

3. _____

Saturday ···············

1. _____

2. _____

3. _____

Wednesday ·············

1. _____

2. _____

3. _____

Sunday ·················

1. _____
2. _____
3. _____

Thursday ···············

1. _____
2. _____
3. _____

Monday ················

1. _____
2. _____
3. _____

Friday ·················

1. _____
2. _____
3. _____

Tuesday ···············

1. _____
2. _____
3. _____

Saturday ···············

1. _____
2. _____
3. _____

Wednesday ············

1. _____
2. _____
3. _____

Tip! Put a jar next to your bed with slips of paper next to it to write your three good things from each day. When you're feeling really down one day, open the jar and read the slips of paper to help bring you back up!

Gratitude TREE

This tree is looking pretty bare! Add a leaf each time you think of something that you are thankful for.

When dealing with disappointment, it's healthy to acknowledge your feelings and think of the good things in your life. Coming back to this tree might help!

Gratitude ABC'S

For each letter in the alphabet, fill in something that you are grateful for that begins with that letter:

A. _____   N. _____

B. _____   O. _____

C. _____   P. _____

D. _____   Q. _____

E. _____   R. _____

F. _____   S. _____

G. _____   T. _____

H. _____   U. _____

I. _____   V. _____

J. _____   W. _____

K. _____   X. _____

L. _____   Y. _____

M. _____   Z. _____

SAYING *Thank You*

Write a list of people you'd like to say "Thank You" to (for any reason). Make a hand-written card for them and check off their box below when the card has been sent.

1. _____ ☐
2. _____ ☐
3. _____ ☐
4. _____ ☐
5. _____ ☐
6. _____ ☐
7. _____ ☐
8. _____ ☐
9. _____ ☐
10. _____ ☐
11. _____ ☐
12. _____ ☐

CHAPTER 3

I CAN

Dream Big

You may have heard that if you dream it, you can do it! The truth is this is only partly correct. You can and should have big dreams. This means thinking about what you really want to do or achieve. But it's not quite enough to just dream about it. If all you ever do is dream about it, then it may never become a reality. Setting goals regularly and carefully can help you feel in control of your dreams so that you can take the right steps toward making them come true.

Setting short-term goals for yourself can be a lot of fun and can make you feel super accomplished. The kinds of goals in this section are not based on grades, winning, or other results that are out of our control. Goals based on results can make us feel discouraged, whereas goals based on simply completing tasks can make us feel motivated.

The following activities can help you set goals that will help you get closer to your dreams!

"The future belongs to those who believe in the beauty of their dreams."
ELEANOR ROOSEVELT

Zooming Out

Let's zoom out and think about setting specific goals that stretch you further. For example, if you already eat a healthy breakfast every morning, setting a goal to eat a healthy breakfast might not be necessary. Examine your life from a zoomed-out perspective—one that looks at your goals and how you can accomplish them. These goals may be broader, but they should still be specific and accomplishable, not results-driven.

If I could learn about anything, I would like to learn about:

_____

_____

Here are some ways I can help in my community this year:

_____

_____

Here are some ways I can be a good friend this year:

_____

_____

Here are some ways I can help people less fortunate than me:

_____

_____

Here are some ways I can excel in school:

_____

_____

"Set lofty goals for yourself and believe that with really hard work you can achieve them."

IBTIHAJ MUHAMMAD

NOW LET'S DREAM BIG! Now that you have focused on the process and some smaller goals that you can actively achieve, let's think about a dream goal—one that may not be realized until many years from now!

What is the biggest dream you can possibly imagine?

Some examples may include:

💜 Being in the Olympics

🤍 Becoming a doctor

💙 Going into outer space

💜 Performing on Broadway

No dream is too *wild* or *outrageous!*

MY BIG DREAM IS . . .

_____

_____

_____

_____

_____

_____

_____

DRAW A PICTURE OF YOUR BIGGEST DREAM COMING TRUE
· ·

"Every great dream begins with a dreamer. Always remember, you have within you the strength, the patience, and the passion to reach for the stars to change the world."
HARRIET TUBMAN

"Never doubt that you are valuable and powerful and deserving of every chance and opportunity in the world to pursue and achieve your own dreams."

HILLARY CLINTON

CREATING YOUR Dream LADDER

Write your big dream in the space at the top of the ladder. Achieving this goal will require many steps along the way. Sometimes, obstacles or fear of failure make us turn back around. List some steps you can take to reach your goal. Then, think about the obstacles that may arise and possible solutions for overcoming them.

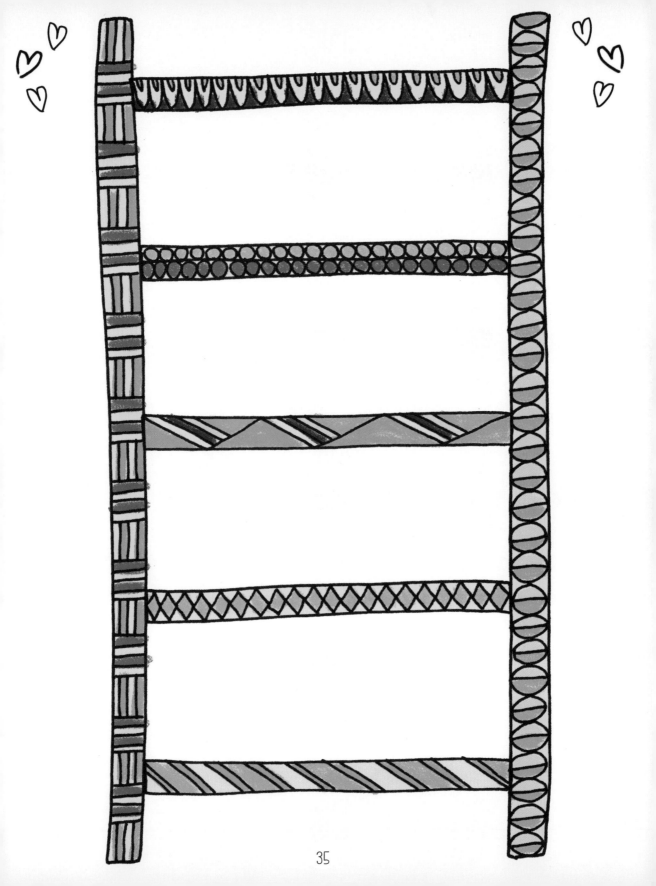

CHAPTER 4

I CAN BE Confident

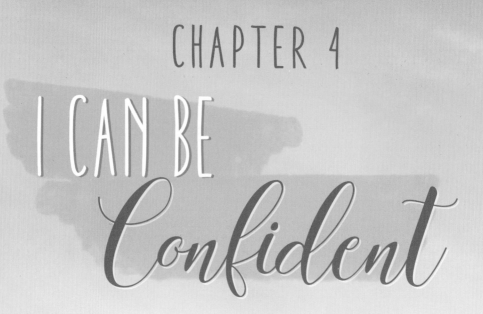

Confidence is a belief in your own abilities and qualities. Developing your confidence helps you try new things, cope with challenges and mistakes, and take pride in who you are and what you've accomplished. Confidence can come as a result of how you think and what you focus on.

You might think confidence is just something you're either born with or not, but that's not true! The following activities will help you understand confidence as something you have control over. Confidence isn't determined by how you feel, but rather by how you think. And if it's a thought, then you are in charge of it!

WAYS TO *Boost* YOUR CONFIDENCE

Sit Up Straight! - Sitting with good posture can lead to confidence in your thoughts, as well as a better mood.

Power Pose! - Do this for at least two minutes a day, every day. (More on power poses in a bit!)

Practice Self-Affirmation! - These are positive statements you can say to yourself to remind you that you're awesome.

Visualize! - Picturing yourself doing well on a presentation or performance can lead to greater feelings of confidence and help prepare your mind for the challenge.

Sweat It Out! - Exercising releases feel-good chemicals in the brain like dopamine and endorphins and can regulate stress hormones like cortisol and adrenaline.

Practice! - Practicing a skill or task can boost your confidence. Practice can lead to progress and improvement with a particular skill, which can in turn make you feel more confident.

Smile, Laugh, And Have Fun! - Like exercise, laughter also releases endorphins, a chemical that makes you feel happy.

Mirror And Model Your Heroes! - How do they act? What habits do they have? How can you learn from them?

COPYING *Confidence*

Identify three role models (people you know personally or just admire from afar) whom you can mimic when you need a confidence boost. Remember, if you can identify a positive quality in others, then you already have some of that in yourself!

1. _____

What I admire about this person: _____

_____

How I can try and be like this person: _____

_____

2. _____

What I admire about this person: _____

_____

How I can try to be like this person: _____

_____

3. _____

What I admire about this person: _____

_____

How I can try to be like this person: _____

_____

"Practice creates confidence. Confidence empowers you." SIMONE BILES

SELF-Love ♥ ....

To develop a habit of positive thinking, start your day off with some self-affirmation. An affirmation is a statement that reveals what's great about you. Write down five self-affirmations in the space below. Examples include "I am kind," "I am enough," "I am beautiful," "I believe in me," etc.

1. _____

2. _____

3. _____

4. _____

5. _____

Repeat these to yourself in the mirror every morning after brushing your teeth! Visualizing your self-affirmations can be incredibly helpful in making you believe in yourself. For example, if your self-affirmation is "I am strong," then you should visualize yourself showing strength.

"It is important to remember that we all have magic inside us."
J.K. ROWLING

Sometimes we don't even notice when we tell ourselves something negative because thinking negatively has become a habit. The good news is we can break this habit. Practice identifying negative thoughts, as well as positive ones, by crossing out the negative thoughts that would make you feel upset or frustrated and circling in the positive thoughts that are likely to fuel feelings of joy.

I can't do it.

I'm not smart.

I am enough for myself and for others.

I'll never conquer this.

I can overcome.

I will keep trying.

This is impossible.

Mistakes help me learn.

Everyone is better than me.

It's too difficult.

I'll try my best.

This stinks!

I am in control of my feelings and reactions.

Create a GO-TO STATEMENT

Before a test in school, a game, or a new activity, it can be helpful to have a go-to statement. A go-to statement is a statement that's prepared ahead of time so that, in a challenging moment, you have something you can say to yourself to give you the confidence boost you need. These statements can be really simple! "I got this!" or "I am ready for this" often do the trick.

Write down three go-to statements in the space below. If you are having trouble creating your statements, think of what your parents or coaches might say when they're giving you a pep talk.

1. _____
_____
_____

2. _____
_____
_____

3. _____
_____
_____

Power POSES ·····································

A power pose is a pose that displays confidence and strength. They can make you feel more confident and less stressed. A typical power pose entails standing up straight and pulling your shoulders back.

Here are some power poses for you to try:

"Don't let anyone define you. You define yourself." BILLIE JEAN KING

Stand in a power pose for two minutes each day or before any big event! See if you notice a difference in how you feel.

Don't like any of these poses? Make up your own! Draw your own unique power pose in the space below:

See IT AND Believe IT!

Picturing yourself in positions of success can help lead to actual success. That's because visualizing positive outcomes can calm your nerves and make you feel excited about the future.

In the space below, draw a picture of yourself conquering one of your biggest fears.

In the space below, draw a picture of yourself trying something new.

In the space below, draw a picture of yourself achieving something you've always wanted.

"It's not the absence of fear. It's overcoming it. Sometimes you've got to blast through and have faith."

EMMA WATSON

CHAPTER 5

I CAN BE

Courageous

Oftentimes people think being courageous or brave means that they are not afraid. BUT, being afraid, nervous, fearful, or scared is totally normal, especially when it comes to standing up for something, trying a new activity, or doing what's right. Having courage just means that you still do all those things in SPITE of being afraid. It means that the fear is still there, but it doesn't control you.

The following activities can help you discover some ways you are already being courageous, and help you become even braver!

FINDING Your COURAGE

Circle the courageous things you have already done.
Underline the things that you haven't done YET but
would like to.

· ·

♡ Learned to ride a bike.

♡ Told the truth
when it was difficult.

♡ Tried a new instrument.

♡ Said thank you to a
clerk at the store
before leaving.

♡ Held a door for
a stranger.

♡ Asked a question in class.

♡ Climbed a rock wall.

♡ Sat with someone new
at lunch.

♡ Made a new friend.

♡ Gave a speech in class.

♡ Learned to cook.

♡ Wrote a thank-you note.

♡ Volunteered.

♡ Learned to swim.

♡ Solved a problem.

♡ Had a difficult talk with a
friend about feelings.

♡ Admitted a mistake.

♡ Shook someone's hand
when meeting them.

♡ Tried a new sport.

"Do one thing that
scares you every day."
ELEANOR ROOSEVELT

WAYS TO *Train Your Courage*

Here are some ways to train your courage. For each, fill out the date you completed it and what you did. Challenge yourself to seek out these experiences!

Today, I tried something new. (New food? New sport? New hobby?)

Date: _____

What happened? _____

_____

_____

How did it make me feel? _____

_____

_____

Today, I traveled to a place I've never been before. (New friend's house? A part of the neighborhood you've never been before? A different city, state, or country?)

Date: _____

What happened? _____

_____

_____

How did it make me feel? _____

_____

_____

Today, I spoke to someone I didn't previously know.

Date: _____

What happened? _____

_____

_____

How did it make me feel? _____

_____

_____

Today, I stood up for myself.

Date: _____

What happened? _____

_____

_____

How did it make me feel? _____

_____

_____

Today, I said something positive about another person—TO THEIR FACE!

Date: _____

What happened? _____

_____

_____

How did it make me feel? _____

_____

_____

FEELING Butterflies

Your body may experience stress in different ways. You might have butterflies in your stomach or you might feel your heart pounding. Your breathing may feel different, such as being short or shallow. Here is the thing—how you think about these physiological responses matters and can transform your experiences with them! Rather than trying to push away the butterflies or the feelings that may come with stress or stressful situations, you can choose to welcome them. You can do this by thinking and knowing that this is simply your body preparing you to meet a challenge. Stress can be your friend when you take this perspective. Whenever you're feeling butterflies in your stomach, think about letting the butterflies fly, and know that this is your body giving you courage to move forward.

"I say I am stronger than fear."
MALALA YOUSAFZAI

In the butterflies, write down some things that give you a stressed-out or nervous feeling when you think about them. These could be certain memories, big upcoming events, or just general unpleasant thoughts.

NOW LET THESE BUTTERFLIES *Fly!*

CHAPTER 6

I CAN *Grow*

"Never give up, for that is just the place and time that the tide will turn."

HARRIET BEECHER STOWE

Our mindset can be thought of as our attitude toward and outlook on life. It has been studied and shown that there are two types of mindsets: a growth mindset and a fixed mindset. In a fixed mindset, people believe their ability, talent, and intelligence are "fixed" traits that cannot be changed. You either have it or you don't! (You are either smart or you're not! You are either talented or you're not!) On the other hand, a growth mindset is the belief that your ability, talent, and intelligence can all grow and be developed through effort and hard work.

Having a growth mindset is an important step to becoming your strongest and happiest self! A growth mindset allows you to embrace feedback and new opportunities while also taking on challenges and facing mistakes. The bottom line is understanding that you have a CHOICE, and you can work on choosing the attitude and mindset that best sets you up for happiness and success.

Fill in the blanks below with your own experiences. Once the sentences are complete, read them out loud to yourself—and keep reading them until you believe them to be true!

I'm not proud of the time that I _____ , but mistakes help me learn.

I'm not the best at _____ , but with practice, I can improve.

I still don't understand _____ , but with patience, I can figure it out.

I really struggle with _____ , but through hard work, it will get easier.

I'm not confident about _____ , but if I keep believing in myself, I will start to feel more secure.

I'm not comfortable with _____ , but the more I do it, the easier it will get.

I'm not excited about _____ , but I will have an open mind about it, and it will be okay.

"Take chances, make mistakes. That's how you grow. Pain nourishes your courage. You have to fail in order to practice being brave."
MARY TYLER MOORE

Practice Makes Progress

One word that can change your attitude is . . . YET! This word leaves room for growth and improvement.

Fill in the following sentences and then add YET to the end of every sentence.

"I'm not good at _____

_____ ."

"I'm not good at _____

_____ ."

"I'm not good at _____

_____ ."

"I'm not good at _____

_____ ."

"I'm not good at _____

_____ ."

"I'm not good at _____

_____ ."

"I am unable to do _____."

"I am unable to do _____."

"I am unable to do _____."

"I am unable to do _____."

"I am unable to do _____."

"I tried _____,
but it didn't work _____."

"I tried _____,
but it didn't work _____."

"I tried _____,
but it didn't work _____."

"I tried _____,
but it didn't work _____."

"I tried _____,
but it didn't work _____."

Hear a friend say they can't do something? Add YET to the end of their sentence for them to encourage them to keep trying!

Understanding CONTROL

"Your success and happiness lies in you. Resolve to keep happy, and your joy and you shall form an invincible host against difficulties." HELEN KELLER

There are so many things in life that we don't have control over, but we can always control how we react to things that happen to us. The way we choose to react to things that are out of our control is what determines our attitude.

Place the phrases below into the correct place in the diagram. The things we can alcontrol should go INSIDE the human shape. The things we can't control should go OUTSIDE. Add more phrases of your own to each section!

♡ The weather

♡ Traffic

♡ What other people say or do

♡ My actions

♡ My behavior

♡ My outlook

♡ My words

♡ How tall I am

♡ Who my biological family members are

♡ Who my friends are

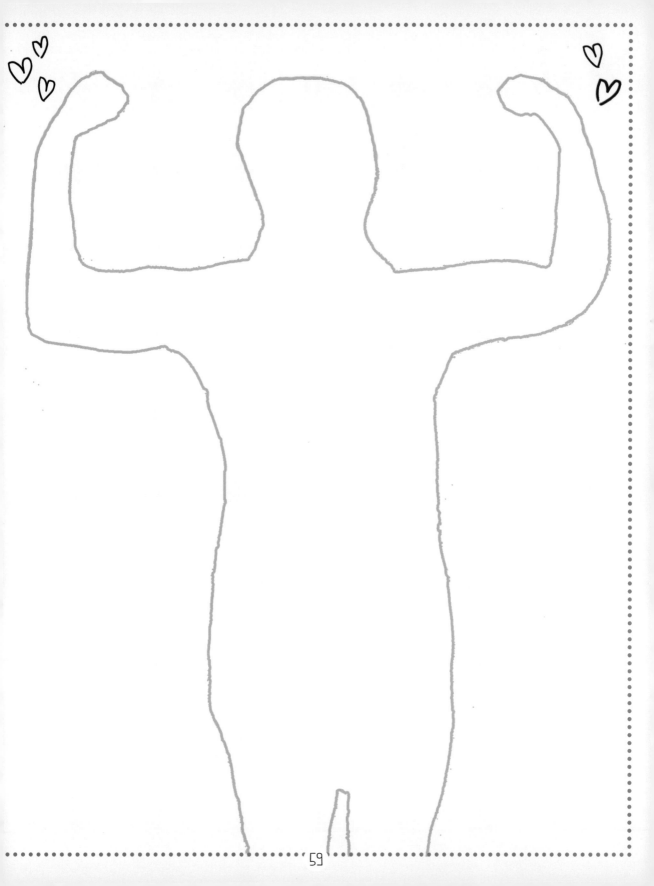

Kindness COUNTS

Did you know that being kind could actually make you into a happier person? It's true! That's because positivity and kindness feed off of each other. In the space below, come up with 10 random acts of kindness to do. Be creative and thoughtful in coming up with these. Look around in your life and think about what others might need. These acts can be as simple as holding the door for someone, sitting with someone new at lunch, or paying someone a compliment.

1. _____

2. _____

3. _____

4. _____

5. _____

6. _____

7. _____

8. _____

9. _____

10. _____

See if you can carry out at least four acts of kindness for four different people (one kind act per person) in the same day.

Let's suppose those four people are inspired by your kindness and decide to also perform four acts of kindness for four people in their own lives. Then, suppose that the next day, those people decide to perform acts of kindness for four people that they know.

If kindness keeps spreading at this rate, here's what the math comes out to:

Day 1 ●●●●●●●●●●●●●●● 4

Day 2 ●●●●●●●●●●●●● 16

Day 3 ●●●●●●●●●●●●● 64

Day 4 ●●●●●●●●●●● 256

Day 5 ●●●●●●●●●● 1,024

Day 6 ●●●●●●●●●●● 4,096

Day 7 ●●●●●●●●● 16,384

Day 8 ●●●●●●●●● 65,536

Day 9 ●●●●●●●● 262,144

Day 10 ●●●●●●●● 1,048,576

That is over *1 MILLION* people experiencing kindness from others in just 10 days! This all started with just a single person—*YOU!*

●●●●●●●●●●●●●●●●●●●●●●●●●●●●

"Carry out random acts of kindness, with no expectation of reward, safe in the knowledge that one day someone might do the same for you."
PRINCESS DIANA

Kindness counts—so don't stop counting the acts of kindness you give and receive.

Use the space below to record these acts of kindness as they occur.

My Acts of Kindness	Date

Acts of Kindness from Others	Date

My Acts of Kindness	Date

Acts of Kindness from Others	Date

My Acts of Kindness   Date

_____

_____

_____

Acts of Kindness from Others   Date

_____

_____

_____

My Acts of Kindness   Date

_____

_____

_____

Acts of Kindness from Others   Date

_____

_____

_____

My Acts of Kindness   Date

_____

_____

_____

Acts of Kindness from Others   Date

_____

_____

CHAPTER 7

I CAN

Fail

"Think like a queen. A queen is not afraid to fail. Failure is another stepping stone to greatness."
OPRAH WINFREY

Did you know that mistakes make your brain grow? This doesn't mean the physical size of your brain grows until it no longer fits in your head (that would be bizarre!). It means, rather, that the part of the brain where learning occurs grows. And not only that, it grows MORE when you make mistakes. When you make mistakes, your brain is entering territory it has never been to before. Sometimes this concept is called "brain plasticity," meaning that your brain can change, grow, and even rewire itself to meet challenges.

The following activities help you process your mistakes and understand the importance of failure.

Mistakes—THE ULTIMATE BRAIN FOOD!

Think of your brain like a muscle. It can get stronger (smarter!) the more we exercise it through trying new things, learning from our mistakes, and dealing with uncertainty. Making mistakes isn't fun, but we wouldn't grow into better people if we didn't mess up sometimes. The kinder we are toward ourselves when we make a mistake or fail, the better we feel about it, and as a result, the more likely we are to recover so we can move on to other things. These other things can open the door to more mistakes, but we shouldn't be afraid of that! As stated before—MISTAKES HELP US GROW!

Write about a time you made a small mistake (choosing the wrong answer on a test, accidentally breaking something, etc.).

_____

_____

Write about what you learned from the experience.

_____

_____

Write about a time when you made a big mistake (hurting a friend, saying something mean to a family member, etc.).

_____

_____

Write about what you learned from the experience.

_____

_____

CAN YOU FEEL YOUR BRAIN GROWING?!

66

Below is a list of mistakes you can make. After each mistake, write down a possible solution or a lesson that could be learned from the experience. By simply thinking through some of these scenarios and jotting your thoughts down, you are already starting the growth process.

I forgot my homework at home.

_____

I was not kind to someone who needed it.

_____

I didn't get the grade I wanted on the project.

_____

I lied.

_____

I didn't help someone who was clearly in need.

_____

I gossiped about someone.

_____

I ignored my responsibilities.

_____

I broke a promise.

_____

TIP! When you make a mistake that hurts others in some way, be sure to acknowledge the mistake and apologize for it! Being able to admit when you have made a mistake is part of being a strong person.

Remember, don't worry or beat yourself up over these mistakes. Your brain had the opportunity to grow because of them!

"Failure happens all the time . . . What makes you better is how you react to it." MIA HAMM

...... Mistakes CAN'T SLOW YOU DOWN!

Just because you've made some mistakes doesn't mean you should stop trying altogether.
Use the next few pages to catalog your mistakes so that you can see how you're constantly growing. Put a check in the box provided to indicate that you've learned from the experience.

♥ MY MISTAKE: _____
_____

DATE: _____
_____

WHAT I LEARNED/HOW I FELT: _____
_____
_____

DID I GROW? _____

♥ MY MISTAKE: _____
_____

DATE: _____
_____

WHAT I LEARNED/HOW I FELT: _____
_____
_____

DID I GROW? _____

♥ MY MISTAKE: _____
_____

DATE: _____
_____

WHAT I LEARNED/HOW I FELT: _____
_____
_____

DID I GROW? _____

♥ MY MISTAKE: _____
_____

DATE: _____
_____

WHAT I LEARNED/HOW I FELT: _____
_____
_____

DID I GROW? _____

♥ MY MISTAKE: _____
_____

DATE: _____
_____

WHAT I LEARNED/HOW I FELT: _____
_____
_____

DID I GROW? _____

FINDING THE *Positive*

Even in moments of failure, there can be a positive side to things. It's all about your perspective and what you choose to make of the situation. In the space provided, keep a running list of the positive outlooks you chose to take when you failed at different things.

MY FAILURES, BIG AND SMALL:	FINDING THE POSITIVE...
My friend and I tried juggling three balls but couldn't.	We laughed a lot and had fun!
I didn't find the jeans I wanted when I went shopping.	I got to spend time at the mall with friends.

MY FAILURES, BIG AND SMALL:	FINDING THE POSITIVE....

CHAPTER 8

I CAN BE Mindful

"For me, the adventures of the mind, each inflection of thought, each movement, nuance, growth, discovery, is a source of exhiliration."

ANAÏS NIN

There are many different definitions of mindfulness. One way to think about it is that mindfulness is awareness. It is noticing what is happening right now (such as noticing your thoughts, feelings, sounds, and senses). By being mindful of what's going on around us and inside of us, we are able to be in the moment, which allows us to really experience the present, rather than worry about the past or the future.

Mindfulness practice can help us:

- ♥ Stress less
- ♥ Worry less
- ♥ Deal with change
- ♥ Sleep better
- ♥ Feel more connected to others
- ♥ Be grateful
- ♥ Be more confident
- ♥ Be better at dealing with problems
- ♥ Perform better in school and other activities
- ♥ Concentrate and focus better
- ♥ Feel content and happy

The following exercises will help you develop mindfulness. Remember—mindfulness isn't an accomplishment or end goal. It's a lifelong practice and a way of being.

Meditation ♡ ♡

What you may think of when you hear the word meditation is someone sitting in lotus position with his or her eyes closed. A common misconception about meditation is that it is when you think about nothing or when your mind is empty. The truth is, an "empty" mind is neither possible nor the goal! Meditating is a specific way to practice being mindful, and often that means our mind is full of lots of thoughts! The goal in meditating is not to become the best meditator in the world. Rather, the goal is to bring greater awareness and perspective to your daily life. This can become a powerful tool, especially in times of stress. While it is not always relaxing to meditate (it can be, but sometimes it's just really hard and not relaxing at all!), with time it builds your mental strength and ability to deal with difficult situations.

There are essentially four phases to a meditation:

PHASE 1: Find your meditation anchor, something you can focus on while you're meditating. The most common anchor is your breath. Other anchors include the feeling of your body on the ground or in the chair, counting, or listening to sounds in the room.

PHASE 2: Undoubtedly, your attention will wander away from your anchor. You might start thinking about what you want to eat for dinner or an event that happened that day.

PHASE 3: You become aware that your mind has wondered.

PHASE 4: You bring your attention back to your anchor.

Then, the cycle starts all over again!

Try a simple meditation involving your breath. Set a timer for 60 seconds and get in a comfortable place. You can choose to sit on the floor, in a chair with your feet on the ground in front of you, or even lie down. After you hit "start" on your timer, gently close your eyes and begin paying attention to your breath. Focus on inhaling and exhaling. You can even say "in" and "out" as you breathe. When you notice your mind has wandered, don't worry! Just bring your attention back to each breath. Continue doing this until your timer goes off.

As you get more comfortable with this practice, you can add more minutes to your timer! Remember, meditation is a practice. The more you do it, the more you are strengthening your mindfulness muscle!

Use the space below to journal each time you meditate. Writing about your experience is another way to bring greater awareness to the process.

• •

Date: _____

Minutes of Meditating: _____

How I felt before: _____

_____

_____

How I felt during: _____

_____

_____

How I felt after: _____

_____

_____

Date: _____

Minutes of Meditating: _____

How I felt before: _____

_____

_____

How I felt during: _____

_____

_____

How I felt after: _____

_____

_____

Date: _____

Minutes of Meditating: _____

How I felt before: _____

_____

_____

How I felt during: _____

_____

_____

How I felt after: _____

_____

_____

Date: _____

Minutes of Meditating: _____

How I felt before: _____

_____

_____

How I felt during: _____

_____

_____

How I felt after: _____

_____

_____

Mindful PRACTICES

Like everything, becoming more aware of our thoughts and feelings and being in the moment takes practice. Sitting meditation is one great way to practice mindfulness, but it's not the only way. Below are some mindfulness exercises to try on your own.

Here are a few ways to practice that do not involve a sitting meditation:

♥ **Mindfulness In Nature**— Go outside and sit in nature. (Your backyard or a park will do just fine!) Try to tune into all your senses. Write down everything you see. Write down everything you hear. Write down everything you smell.

_____

_____

_____

_____

_____

♥ **Mindful Walking**— Go outside if you can (inside will work also) and walk just to walk, without the purpose of getting anywhere. Gaze at the ground or floor in front of your feet and notice the sensation of your feet stepping on the ground, one foot after the other. As your mind wanders, keep coming back to the feeling of one foot in front of the other. What did you notice? What was distracting? How did you feel?

_____

_____

_____

_____

_____

♥ **Brushing Your Teeth**— When you brush your teeth, pay attention to the sounds, smells, taste, and feeling with each brush. When you notice you've started thinking about something else, bring your attention back to simply brushing your teeth. What sounds did you hear? What did it taste like? What did you smell?

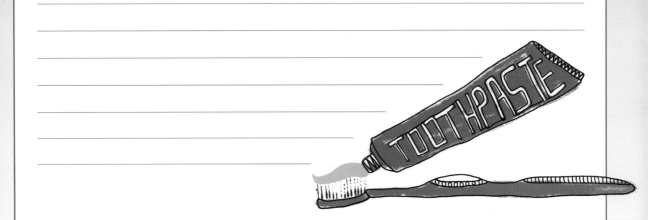

♥ **Ice Cube Exercise**— Hold an ice cube while it melts in your hand. Put a paper towel down or stand above a sink. You will notice your hand getting cold, maybe even painful. Try to keep your attention on what it feels like without dropping the ice cube. See if you can hold the ice cube until it melts completely. Take a break if you need to, but then try to pick it back up again and finish the exercise. What sensations did you feel in your hand? How did you focus your attention when the ice cube got really cold?

♥ **Eating A Raisin** — We will try to engage all the senses again. Hold onto a raisin and start by looking at it. Really look at it closely, like you have never seen a raisin before! Touch it and notice the sensation and what it feels like. After exploring the raisin through touch and sight, smell it. Finally, put it in your mouth and chew it, paying attention to the sounds, feelings, and taste of the raisin. Lastly, swallow it, noticing what your body did in order to swallow it. See if you can pay attention to the feeling of the raisin going down. What did the raisin feel like in your hand? Can you provide details of what the raisin looked like? What did the raisin feel like in your mouth? Can you describe how the raisin tastes?

_____

_____

_____

_____

_____

♥ **Finding A New Vantage Point** — Try seeing things from a different point of view—literally! If you always sit in the same seat in your classroom or at the dinner table, find a different seat, if possible. Observe the room you are in from this new seat and notice as many things as you can. What is different about the space from this new angle? Do you like this new point of view better or worse? Why?

_____

_____

_____

_____

_____

WHEN IN DOUBT—*Color It Out!*

Grab your coloring pencils and take your time coloring this design however you'd like. Coloring is an easy way to get into a flow where your attention is focused only on the design and the act. Coloring can help you bring your mind to a state of inner calm and can be both a soothing and fun activity.

Responding INSTEAD OF REACTING

When bringing greater mindfulness to your daily life, you will find that you are able to choose to respond instead of react to events. Sometimes there are events or actions that may provoke a reaction from you. When something unexpected or upsetting happens, take a breath, remind yourself to be mindful, and then respond.

> For example, if you spill your drink on the floor, you could react by getting mad and frustrated. Or, you could take a breath and then respond by getting towels to clean it up.
>
> Add to this list things of events that could provoke reactions and write down how you will respond instead:
>
> ♥ Someone interrupted me when I was talking → Deep breath → Response:
>
> _____
>
> ♥ I didn't finish first in a competition → Deep breath → Response:
>
> _____
>
> ♥ _____
>
> _____
>
> ♥ _____
>
> _____
>
> ♥ _____
>
> _____

UNPLUG AND UNWIND

In our modern world that's full of screens everywhere, it's really important to unplug from technology. Research shows that time away from technology helps you focus and sleep better. Consider trying any one of these 30 activities for at least ten minutes when you're in need of a break. Cross out the ones you've completed as you go!

- Impromptu dance party!
- Read a book.
- Take a walk outside.
- Take a nap.
- Write a letter to a friend.
- Take a bath.
- Color.
- Go for a bike ride.
- Listen to music.
- Stretch.
- Go for a run.
- Create your own fun and funny exercise routine.
- Take some deep belly breaths.
- Play with a pet.
- Meditate.
- Play a board game.
- Jump rope.

- Paint.
- Bake a dessert.
- Lie on the ground outside and watch the clouds go by.
- Cook.
- Sing your favorite tunes.
- Doodle.
- Pick flowers.

- Jump in leaves.
- Do a craft.
- Spend some time near water (beach, lake, pool, river, etc.)
- Be silly.
- Paint your nails.
- Decorate your room.

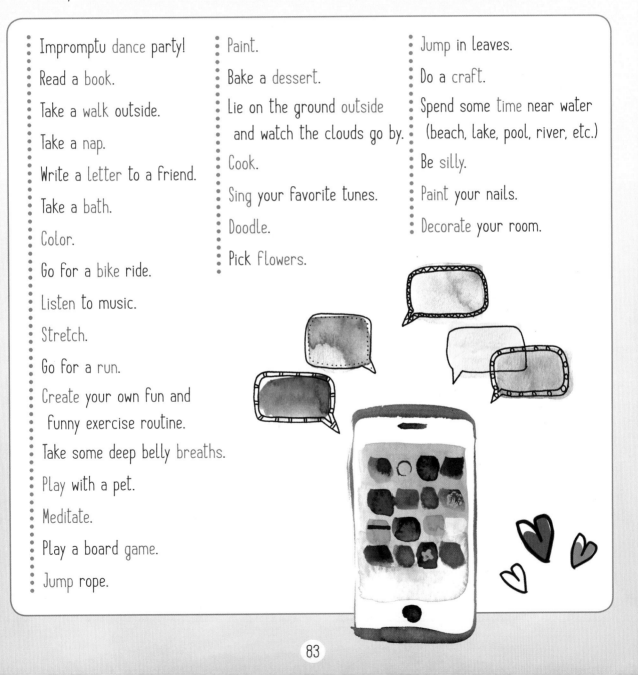

TEST YOUR BREATH

Our breath helps us regulate our emotions and is another way to practice mindfulness. When we breathe deeply in and out, it can reduce our heart rate, which could help us deal with stressful situations.

Let's first test your breath. Put one hand on your chest and one hand on your belly. Take slow, deep breaths. Which hand is moving? The hand on your belly should be where most of the action occurs. Sometimes it is easier to test your breath by lying down. So, let's try it now. Lie down comfortably and put a lightweight magazine or a stuffed animal on your belly. Take some slow, deep breaths and try to focus on raising the magazine or stuffed animal. Learning to breathe in this way can help your performance and is a resource to reduce stress and/or tension. Have you ever noticed a baby breathing? You see the baby's belly rise and fall. Retrain yourself to breathe like a baby! Like everything in this book, the more you practice it, the better you will get. Your deep belly breathing can then become your first resource to calm yourself in difficult or stressful situations. Using your breath properly is also a way to help you manage your emotions. Why is it your first resource? Because you always have your breath with you everywhere you go!

Breathing EXERCISES TO PRACTICE

In and Out - Sit or lie down comfortably and focus on your breath. Each time a thought or distraction (such as other noises) come into your mind, just bring your attention back to your breathing. To help, some people will like to say the word "in" silently when taking a breath in and "out" when breathing out.

Counting Breaths - When you breathe in, try to relax your body and on the slow breath out silently count "one." Then repeat feeling your body relax when you breathe in and breathe out counting "two" until your lungs are empty. Continue this process. It can help you stay focused by closing your eyes during this exercise. If you lose count of your breaths because your mind has wandered, just start back at "one" again.

Stuffed Animal - Put a stuffed animal on your belly and take some breaths watching the stuffed animal go up and down.

Back-to-Back - Sit back to back with a friend and pay attention to feeling the breaths they are taking. See if you can tell when they are breathing in and when they are breathing out.

Bubbles - Blow (or pretend to blow) bubbles trying to breathe out as long and slow as possible.

Smelling - Pretend to be smelling a flower, slowly breathing in through your nose and then slowly breathing out through your mouth.

Tip! One "formula" to use, if it is helpful, is 4-2-5. Breathe in for 4 seconds, hold for 2, and then breathe out for 5 seconds. Remember to feel your breath from your belly. As you get older, you can practice breathing in and out for longer.

Just BREATHE

After some practice focusing on your breath, answer the following questions:

Is it hard or easy paying attention to your breath? _____
_____

How do you feel after? _____
_____
_____

What's your favorite breathing exercise? _____
_____
_____

Write down some situations where just
breathing could help you feel better.

_____
_____
_____
_____
_____

BUBBLES

Draw a picture of when you have or could have used deep belly breathing to help you feel better.

CHAPTER 9

I CAN Love Myself

"You alone are enough. You have nothing to prove to anybody."
MAYA ANGELOU

Have you ever been really upset with yourself? Maybe you fell short of your own expectations, or maybe things didn't go the way you originally planned. That's where self-compassion comes in. Self-compassion is being kind and gentle towards yourself, particularly in moments of frustration or disappointment. In other words, it means giving yourself a little love!

Self-compassion can lead to . . .

- Better relationships with others.
- An ideal state of mind, which allows us to be our best.
- More perseverance when faced with obstacles.
- More confidence.
- More motivation.
- More happiness.

Compassion is when you understand what others are going through and want to be kind and help them. Self-compassion means that you are the one going through something, and you extend kindness and helpfulness to yourself. Sometimes it's obvious to care for others, but we often forget that we need to give that same care to ourselves.

The fact of the matter is, no one is perfect! Reminding yourself of this is the first step to figuring out how you can best love yourself. The following activities will also help with that!

LOVE FOR *You*, LOVE FOR *Me*

Think of people that you would like to send kind and loving thoughts to. Fill in the blanks below with names of those people.

I wish to send love to _____.

I wish to send kindness to _____.

I wish to send happy thoughts to _____.

I hope _____ is content.

I hope _____ is healthy.

I hope _____ feels at peace.

Repeat the same exercise—but this time, fill in the blanks with your name! A huge part of self-compassion is treating yourself like you would a loved one or someone close to you.

I wish to send love to _____.

I wish to send kindness to _____.

I wish to send happy thoughts to _____.

I hope _____ is content.

I hope _____ is healthy.

I hope _____ feels at peace.

Think about when a friend feels really down about him- or herself and is stuck in a bad mood. Make a list below of some things you might say or do to help them feel better?

Let's go get ice cream! _____

Let's do a fun activity. _____

_____

_____

_____

Now when YOU are feeling down or stuck in a bad mood, consider saying or doing these things for yourself. Remember, the key to self-compassion is treating yourself like you would a loved one or friend.

Now make a list of different things that you appreciate about yourself. These can be talents, skills, or aspects of your personality.

_____   _____

_____   _____

_____   _____

_____   _____

_____   _____

WE'RE ALL IN THIS *Together*

Write down your name in the center bubble. In the other bubbles, write down the names of people in your life. They could be friends, family, or anyone you feel close to! Finally, draw lines, bridges, paw prints, or anything you'd like to connect your bubble to everyone else's. When you're feeling down or lonely, come back to this image to remind yourself that you're not alone. Everyone feels sad or lonely at times—and that's okay! It is part of what makes us all human!

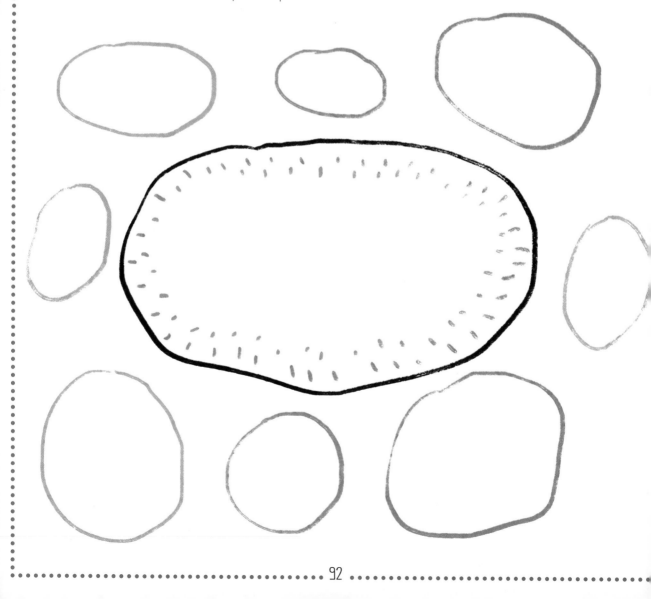

CHAPTER 10

I CAN

Lead

FOLLOW ME!

> *"Don't follow the crowd, let the crowd follow YOU."*
> MARGARET THATCHER

· ·

Each of the topics you have covered so far in this journal are things you can continually work on to develop your leadership skills. A leader is someone who makes positive choices and brings people together. Leaders also use their strengths to solve problems and resolve conflicts. Everyone can be a leader through their actions and how they influence others.

The following activities will encourage you to think about what it takes to be a leader and set goals for ways in which you can make a difference.

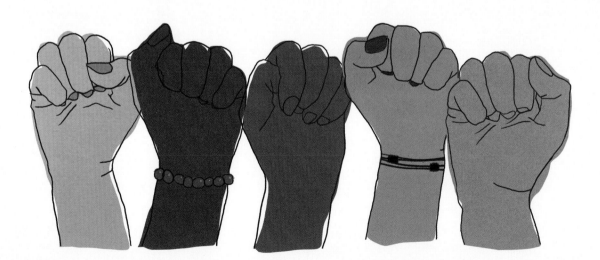

DO YOU HAVE WHAT IT TAKES? (Yes!)

The words below describe qualities that leaders have. Circle the ones that best describe you.

- ♥ Optimistic
- ♥ Curious
- ♥ Helpful
- ♥ Brave
- ♥ Considerate
- ♥ Honest
- ♥ Passionate
- ♥ Creative

- ♥ Hopeful
- ♥ Loving
- ♥ Attentive
- ♥ Kind
- ♥ Generous
- ♥ Giving
- ♥ Trustworthy
- ♥ Confident

- ♥ Supportive
- ♥ Determined
- ♥ Motivated
- ♥ Open-Minded
- ♥ Encouraging
- ♥ Clever
- ♥ Patient
- ♥ Funny

If you circled at least a couple words, then congratulations—you already have what it takes to be a leader! But even leaders can improve and become better leaders. Put a box around the qualities that you wish you had or that you know you could improve on.

"The most effective way to do it is to do it." AMELIA EARHART

"What you do makes a
difference, and you have to
decide what kind of difference
you want to make."
JANE GOODALL

In the space below, make a loose plan for practicing one of the qualities that
you boxed.

I can be more _____ . Here's how: _____

_____

_____

_____

_____

_____

_____

_____

_____

_____

_____

_____

_____

_____

_____

_____

_____

WHAT DOES A LEADER LOOK LIKE?

Understanding yourself helps you grow as a leader. Draw a self-portrait in the space below. Then, cut out pictures from magazines of things that you like or that mean something to you. You can also print pictures from the Internet. Paste these images around your drawing to make a collage.

YOU LOOK *Fabulous!*

THEIR STRENGTHS CAN BE MY STRENGTHS ········

Who is someone that you view as a leader? This person can be someone you know, a historical figure, or a current celebrity. In the space below, write down the qualities that you think make this person a leader. Be as specific or as general as you want.

_____ is an awesome leader because he/she:

_____

_____

_____

_____

_____

In what ways are you similar to this person? How are you different? Are there things you can do to become more like him/her? Jot your thoughts down in the space below.

_____

_____

_____

_____

_____

"I believe great people do things before they are ready." AMY POEHLER

Great LEADERS MAKE MISTAKES

Leaders are not perfect! But they do learn from their mistakes.

After making a mistake, leaders often:

1. Own the mistake.

2. Forgive themselves (self-compassion!).

3. Learn from their mistake.

4. Make a plan so the same mistake doesn't happen again.

5. Keep trying new things—even if more mistakes could happen!

Think of a time that you made a mistake and fill in the blanks below.

One time, I _____ ,

but I forgive myself. From my mistake, I learned that _____

_____

_____ .

Next time, to avoid making this mistake, I'll be sure to _____

_____

_____

I'm still a strong and capable person.

· *Onward!*

"None of us can know what we are capable of until we are tested."
ELIZABETH BLACKWELL

PLANNING AHEAD ....

Leaders are often bold and take initiative. Sometimes we call this being proactive. This means planning ahead and finding ways that you can make an impact. You can be proactive in large ways, like starting an extracurricular club at school, or in small ways, like cleaning your room without having to be told.

What are three ways you could be proactive at your school? Think: What could make school a better place for everyone?

_____

_____

_____

What are three ways you could be proactive in your community? Think: Is there something your community is missing?

_____

_____

_____

What are five ways you could be proactive in your home? Think: Is there a need that you could fill?

_____

_____

_____

_____

_____

Some possibilities include:
- Picking up litter.
- Running a food or book drive for those in need.

- Setting the table for dinner.
- Cleaning your room.
- Going to bed at a good time to get enough sleep, even when you like staying up.

EMPOWERING *Others*

The best leaders are those who empower others. To empower someone means to lift that person up, to make them feel seen, heard, and valued. You do this first by paying attention to the people around you. What are they good at? Are there traits in them that you admire?

YOU CAN DO IT !

I BELIEVE IN YOU

Choose to empower others rather than bring them down. When you talk about others, highlight what you appreciate about them and their positive qualities, not their weaknesses and mistakes.

You can empower anyone, but it might be easier to start with someone you know. Fill in the blanks below, keeping in mind someone you admire. Think about this person's specifics (what they're good at, what makes them stand out, etc.).

I think _____ is great for the following reasons:

1. _____

2. _____

3. _____

Now, here's the hard part: It's not empowerment unless you actually tell this person how you feel about them! Be brave and go for it!!!

"Leadership is about making others better as a result of your presence and making sure that impacts lasts in your absence."

SHERYL SANDBERG

CHAPTER 11

I CAN BE
Healthy

"My motivation has always been health—eating healthy and taking care of myself."
GABRIELLE REECE

• •

Being healthy is as much physical as it is mental. You can be healthy by nourishing your body with food and exercise. You can be healthy through making safe choices for your body. You can also be healthy by treating yourself as kindly as possible.

The mind and the body are linked. We need both to be strong in order to live healthy lives. The following pages give you additional tips and reminders to maintain a healthy body and mind.

HEALTH TIPS FOR *Strong Girls*

MOVE YOUR BODY

Exercising and being active help strengthen your muscles, immune system, and heart. Plus, they boost your energy, help you concentrate, and brighten your mood. Whenever you have the chance: dance, walk, swim, hike, skate, ski, bike, run, and take the stairs instead of the elevator!

What are your favorite activities that get you to move your body?

_____

_____

_____

How can you move your body more on a daily basis?

_____

_____

_____

EAT YOUR FRUITS AND VEGGIES

Your body and mind are constantly growing, and to get the best out of them, you need to fuel yourself with proper nutrition. When you eat healthy, you maintain your energy, improve your skin and bone health, and quite simply feel better!

Think about eating the rainbow. Foods that are bright colors are often some of the best for you, which means that you've got to eat your fruits and veggies.

What are your favorite fruits and vegetables?

_____

_____

_____

_____

Think of your latest meal. Write down all the colors you ate. (If there aren't that many colors, try eating more for your next meal!)

_____

_____

_____

_____

_____

_____

CHOOSE H2O (WATER!)

Drink plenty of water! Water helps regulate your body temperature, aides in digestion, and replaces what is lost when you sweat. Sugary drinks like juice, soda, and sports drinks are fine as an occasional treat, but they don't hydrate your body the way water does. Hydration is tricky because you could be dehydrated even when you don't feel thirsty! But here's a helpful tip: When you are properly hydrated, your pee should be clear (not yellow)! If your pee is very yellow, then it probably means you should be drinking more water.

You should be drinking somewhere between five and seven 8oz glasses of water a day. This amount varies between people, and it would be good to ask your doctor about the proper amount of water intake for you.

For one day, record your water intake by coloring in the glasses below. Remember—sugary drinks don't count! At your next doctor's visit, tell your doctor how many glasses you drank and ask him or her if it's enough.

GET YOUR Z'S

Sleep affects your growth and keeps you from getting sick. It also helps your brain learn and remember new things. It is important to get a good amount of sleep every night in order to maintain a healthy lifestyle. You should listen to your body and get a feel for what you need!

Record how many hours of sleep you've had each night for a week. Make notes about how you felt the following day to see if the amount of sleep you get actually affects how you feel.

♡ MONDAY

Hours of sleep I got: _____

How I felt the next day: _____

♡ TUESDAY

Hours of sleep I got: _____

How I felt the next day: _____

♡ WEDNESDAY

Hours of sleep I got: _____

How I felt the next day: _____

♡ THURSDAY

Hours of sleep I got: _____

How I felt the next day: _____

♡ FRIDAY

Hours of sleep I got: _____

How I felt the next day: _____

♡ SATURDAY

Hours of sleep I got: _____

How I felt the next day: _____

♡ SUNDAY

Hours of sleep I got: _____

How I felt the next day: _____

♡ MONDAY

Hours of sleep I got: _____

How I felt the next day: _____

♡ TUESDAY

Hours of sleep I got: _____

How I felt the next day: _____

♡ WEDNESDAY

Hours of sleep I got: _____

How I felt the next day: _____

♡ THURSDAY

Hours of sleep I got: _____

How I felt the next day: _____

♡ FRIDAY

Hours of sleep I got: _____

How I felt the next day: _____

♡ SATURDAY

Hours of sleep I got: _____

How I felt the next day: _____

♡ SUNDAY

Hours of sleep I got: _____

How I felt the next day: _____

♡ MONDAY

Hours of sleep I got: _____

How I felt the next day: _____

♡ TUESDAY

Hours of sleep I got: _____

How I felt the next day: _____

♡ WEDNESDAY

Hours of sleep I got: _____

How I felt the next day: _____

♡ THURSDAY

Hours of sleep I got: _____

How I felt the next day: _____

♡ FRIDAY

Hours of sleep I got: _____

How I felt the next day: _____

♡ SATURDAY

Hours of sleep I got: _____

How I felt the next day: _____

♡ SUNDAY

Hours of sleep I got: _____

How I felt the next day: _____

Do you recognize a pattern? Does the amount of sleep you get the night before affect your day?
If you want, keep doing this in a separate journal that you designate as your sleep diary!

SURROUND YOURSELF WITH *Awesome* PEOPLE

Being around positive and supportive people is important for your health and happiness! Fill in the blanks below with the names of people who fit the scenario. If you can't think of anyone for a scenario, leave it blank and come back to it later once you've found that person.

Someone I go to if I'm sad: _____

Someone that makes me laugh: _____

Someone I go to for advice: _____

Someone who listens: _____

Someone I share my thoughts with: _____

Someone who understands me: _____

Someone who gives the best hugs: _____

Someone who always wants to have fun: _____

"Never underestimate the power of dreams and the influence of the human spirit. We are all the same in this notion: the potential for greatness lives within each of us."

WILMA RUDOLPH

All About The Women

WHO ARE THE WOMEN QUOTED IN THIS JOURNAL?

MADELEINE ALBRIGHT (1937—) was the first woman to become the United States Secretary of State. She served in this role from 1997–2001. She also served as a university professor from 1982–1993 and authored a number of books. She was awarded the Presidential Medal of Freedom in 2012.

LOUISA MAY ALCOTT (1832–1888) was an American author best known for her novel *Little Women*. She also worked as a teacher and a nurse.

MAYA ANGELOU (1928–2014) was an American author and civil rights activist. Through her poetry, writing, and organizing, she helped rally many Americans to fight discrimination against African-Americans and demand equality for all people.

SIMONE BILES (1997—) is the most decorated American gymnast in history. The winner of 19 Olympic and World Championship medals, Simone also set a record in 2016 for the most gold medals (4) won in women's gymnastics in a single Olympic Games.

ELIZABETH BLACKWELL (1821–1910) moved to the U.S. from England and became the first woman in America to earn a medical degree (from Geneva Medical College in upstate New York) in 1849. Elizabeth founded a medical college to train female doctors in the late 1860s and was a pioneer in enabling women in the medical field.

HILLARY CLINTON (1941—) is a politician. She was the First Lady of the U.S. (1993-2001), the first female U.S. Senator elected from New York (2001-2009), and the Secretary of State (2009-2013). In 2016, she became the first female U.S. presidential nominee for a major political party.

RACHEL CARSON (1907-1964) was a marine biologist, environmentalist, writer, and activist. Her life's work was about preserving the world for future generations. In one of her books, *Silent Spring*, she wrote about the environmental impact of fertilizers and pesticides. She was awarded the Presidential Medal of Freedom in 1980.

MISTY COPELAND (1982—) is an American ballerina. She was the first female African American principal dancer for the prestigious American Ballet Theatre—and she only started dancing at the age of 13! Misty was named as one of TIME Magazine's "100 Most Influential People" in 2015.

ELLEN DEGENERES (1958—) is an American stand-up comedian, actress, and current host of her own talk show, *Ellen*. She is an advocate for equal rights and freedom for everyone. In November of 2016 she received the Presidential Medal of Freedom from President Obama for her contribution to the arts. Among other roles in movies and TV shows, she is the voice of Dory in the movies *Finding Nemo* and *Finding Dory*.

PRINCESS DIANA (1961-1997) was known for her charitable efforts, particularly toward the homeless and children. She was not afraid to speak out and support those whom she felt were mistreated. She is known as a true humanitarian (a person who seeks to support human goodness).

AMELIA EARHART (1897–1938) was an American aviation pioneer and author. She was the first female to fly an airplane solo across the Atlantic Ocean. At the time, she was only the sixth woman to be issued a pilot's license.

TAVI GEVINSON (1996–) is an American writer and actress. She started a fashion blog at age 11, and in 2011 she launched a site for teen girls called *Rookie* (at age 15!). The site had over 1 million views in just the first five days of launching. In her writing, Tavi encourages everyone to be themselves, however quirky and complex that may be.

JANE GOODALL (1934–) is a scientist, animal rights activist, and conservationist. She grew up loving animals and nature. Her love led her to begin studying chimpanzees in Africa, where she interacted with them in the wild while making groundbreaking discoveries! In 1977 she established the Jane Goodall Institute, a global community conservation organization to protect chimpanzees and conserve the natural world.

MIA HAMM (1972–) is a retired professional soccer player. She is a two-time Olympic gold medalist and World Cup winner. In junior high school, she played on the boys' team. She held the record for most international goals for men and women until Abby Wombach beat that record in 2013. The Nike Headquarters in Oregon named a building after her.

MAE JEMISON (1956–) has been a dancer, doctor, astronaut, social scientist, and engineer. In 1992, she became the first African American female to travel into space. Dr. Jemison continues to advocate for getting women and minority students into science programs.

JACKIE JOYNER-KERSEE (1962–) was an Olympic heptathlete (that means she competed in seven track and field events!). She won the silver medal in the heptathlon in the 1984 Olympics. She has won a total of three gold, one silver, and two bronze medals from four different Olympic Games. She accomplished these feats while having severe asthma. She is known as one of the greatest athletes of all time.

HELEN KELLER (1880–1968) was an American author and political activist. At 19 months old, she fell ill and became deaf and blind, but she didn't let that stop her from pursuing her dreams. In 1904, she graduated from college, which made her the first deaf and blind person to earn a Bachelor of Arts degree. She campaigned for women's right to vote, among other things. She is known today as a major advocate for people with disabilities.

BILLIE JEAN KING (1943–) is an American tennis legend. She founded the Women's Sports Foundation in 1974, an active organization that advocates for women in sports. She is famous for her defeat of Bobby Riggs in 1973, in what was called the "Battle of the Sexes." Bobby Riggs said he could beat any woman in a tennis match, but Billie Jean King felt differently. They competed and she won the match in three straight sets in front of a crowd of 30,000 people. She was named one of LIFE Magazine's 20th Century "100 Most Important Americans" in 1990.

MARY TYLER MOORE (1936–2017) was an actress and producer born in Brooklyn, New York. She was an activist and advocate for organizations such as the Humane Society and the Juvenile Diabetes Research Foundation. She is both an Emmy and Tony Award winner as well as the recipient of the Screen Actors Guild lifetime achievement award. She was progressive, forward thinking, and had a great impact on feminism and women's rights, particularly in how women were portrayed on television.

IBTIHAJ MUHAMMAD (1985—) is an American fencer. She was Muslim Sportswoman of the Year in 2012 and named as one of TIME Magazine's "100 Most Influential People" in 2016. Ibtihaj made history at the 2016 Olympic Games in Rio by becoming the first U.S. woman to compete in the Olympics wearing a hijab (a type of head covering worn by some Muslim women), and she earned a bronze medal. She serves as an ambassador on the U.S. Department of State's Empowering Women and Girls Through Sport Initiative.

ANAÏS NIN (1903—1977) was a French-American writer known for her essays, novels, short stories, and journals.

MICHELLE OBAMA (1964—) is a lawyer, writer, and activist. She was also First Lady of the U.S. from 2009 to 2017. In 2010, she launched Let's Move!, a campaign to get healthy food into schools and promote physical activity among kids. In 2014, she launched Let Girls Learn, an initiative to help girls around the world go to school and stay in school. She continues various advocacy initiatives.

AMY POEHLER (1971—) is an actress, comedian, director, producer, and writer. She is also one of the founders of "Amy Poehler's Smart Girls," an organization and website dedicated empowering young girls.

GABRIELLE REECE (1970—) is a 6'3" model, fitness expert, author, and former professional beach volleyball player. She was Nike's first female athlete to design a shoe. She wrote a best-selling book in 2014, *My Foot Is Too Big for the Glass Slipper: A Guide to the Less Than Perfect Life*. She encourages young girls to have a healthy relationship with their bodies.

ELEANOR ROOSEVELT (1884–1962) was a writer, activist, and wife of the 32nd President of the U.S., Franklin Delano Roosevelt. She is the longest serving First Lady in U.S. history (12 years!). Among many other efforts, she fought for expanding the roles of women in the workplace and for the civil rights of African Americans, Asian Americans, and World War II refugees (people forced to leave their country due to unliveable conditions, such as war).

J.K. ROWLING (1965–) is a British writer and film producer. She is the author of the Harry Potter series. The seven books, in total, have sold over 450 million copies, and the movies repeatedly broke box office records. She is the first and, as of 2017, only billionaire author.

WILMA RUDOLPH (1940–1994) was an Olympic champion and track and field icon, both in America and worldwide. She was the first American woman to win three gold medals in a single Olympics, competing in the 100- and 200-meter sprints and the 4x100-meter relay. All of these accomplishments came after she had polio as a child and became paralyzed in one leg. Her doctors told her she wouldn't be able to walk again, but Wilma proved them wrong. In the 1960s, she became recognized as one of the fastest women in the world.

SHERYL SANDBERG (1969–) is a technology executive, author, and activist. She is the Chief Operating Officer of Facebook and founder of leanin.org. She was named in 2012 as one of TIME magazine's most influential people in the world. She advocates for women to earn equal pay and for women to enter more roles in leadership positions.

HARRIET BEECHER STOWE (1811–1896) was an author and social activist. Her most popular novel was *Uncle Tom's Cabin*, which hugely influenced the anti-slavery movement. She dedicated much of her life, even after the Civil War, to writing and advocating for human rights as well as social and political issues.

PAT SUMMITT (1952–2016) was a women's basketball coach at the University of Tennessee. As of 2017, she was the winningest coach in NCAA Division I basketball history (men's and women's!). She won two Olympic medals, the first as a player in 1976 and the second as a coach in 1984. She was awarded the Presidential Medal of Freedom in 2012.

MARGARET THATCHER (1925–2013) was a British stateswoman who served as the Prime Minister of the United Kingdom from 1979 to 1990. She was the longest-serving British Prime Minister of the 20th century and the first woman to have held the office.

HARRIET TUBMAN (1820–1913) was a civil rights activist. She was born into slavery but escaped in 1849. She became famous for her efforts in the Underground Railroad, risking her own life to help people escape to freedom. She was also active in the women's suffrage movement (the movement for women's right to vote).

EMMA WATSON (1990–) is a humanitarian and actress best known for her role as Hermione Granger in the Harry Potter films. She also serves as a United Nations Women's Ambassador and dedicates her efforts toward female empowerment. She is also a huge voice in environmentalism (preserving the environment) and is known for wearing recyclable clothing.

SERENA WILLIAMS (1981—) is an American professional tennis player. She was the 2015 Sportsperson of the Year and holds the record for the most tennis Grand Slam titles (male or female!). Her sister, Venus, is also a professional tennis player, and they have played against each other numerous times in professional tournaments. Serena is vocal about having pride in her body and in her strength as an athlete.

OPRAH WINFREY (1954—) is known as a pioneer for women and a talk show host. She was awarded the Presidential Medal of Freedom in 2013. As one of most influential women in the world, she uses her influence and success to change lives and spread good in the world. She has donated millions to charity.

MALALA YOUSAFZAI (1997—) was born in Pakistan. She became an advocate for girls' education as a child and won the Nobel Peace Prize in 2014 at age 17, making her the youngest person to receive the honor. She continues to advocate for the importance of educating girls around the world.

THESE WOMEN CHANGED THE WORLD, AND YOU CAN TOO!

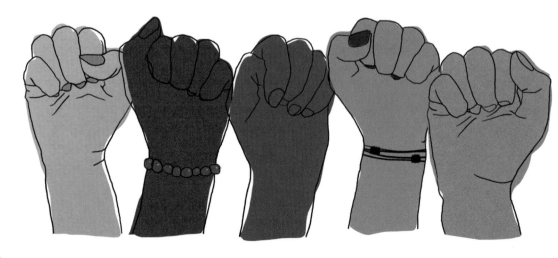

STRONG GIRLS AND WOMEN THAT I LOOK UP TO IN MY LIFE:

_____

_____

_____

_____

_____

_____

_____

_____

_____

_____

_____

_____

_____

Notes AND Reflections